Haiku Roadsign

Haiku Roadsign

A project of Axle Contemporary

Axle Contemporary, Santa Fe, New Mexico

Published by
Axle Contemporary
P.O. Box 22095
Santa Fe, New Mexico 87508

© 2011 Axle Contemporary. All rights reserved.
ISBN 978-0-9858116-2-4
second printing

please visit us at: www.axleart.com

No part of this book may be used or reproduced without permission from the publisher.

Edited and designed by Matthew Chase-Daniel and Jerry Wellman

All photographs by Matthew Chase-Daniel, except pages 6 & 78 by Nina Mastrangelo and page 57 by Jerry Wellman

Special thanks to: Joan Logghe, Laura Addison, Ellen Zieselman, Tim Jag, Joanne Lefrak, Brian Moe, Nina Mastrangelo, Railyard Arts Committee, New Mexico LIterary Arts, those who donated to support this project, the poets, and all of our location partners.

Contents

Axle Contemporary: The Haiku, the Road, the Sign — Jerry Wellman & Matthew Chase-Daniel — 7

Poetry in the Land of Quotidia: The Haiku Roadsign Project — Laura Addison — 8

Drive Slowly: Haiku Zone — Joan Logghe — 10

32 views of the Haiku Roadsign — 12

Poet biographies — 76

Axle Contemporary: The Haiku, the Road, the Sign

Axle Contemporary is a collaboration, a mobile gallery of contemporary art, and a forum to promote and distribute creative projects by artists of many disciplines and all levels of experience.

Last spring, Matthew, while driving his son to school, noticed a forlorn and unused sign leaning against a shed in rural Pojoaque, New Mexico. Over the course of several weeks of repeated sightings, this rusty, dented and faded remnant of another time, transformed into a shining beacon of creative energy.

Matthew brought the kernel of an idea to Jerry and together we created the Axle Contemporary Haiku Roadsign Project. Soon we issued a statewide call for Haiku and invited Santa Fe's Poet Laureate Joan Logghe to jury the entries: 32 poems, 16 weeks, 16 locations.

With this book we demonstrate how a humble, manufactured metal and plastic portable billboard came to travel great distances, through the streets of Santa Fe and through the reaches of people's imaginations.

Haiku printed on paper, collected in a book, evoke the rich experience that can be gained from taking notice of our environment. A poem broadcast on a roadside sign is distinctly different. Reading a haiku while hurtling through space in a car or on a bicycle, while feeling, hearing, and smelling the road, might be more shocking, unexpected, immediate and reverberating. We hope that the joy of discovery inherent in the Haiku Roadsign Project continues to abide in this book.

Art can happen anywhere: In galleries and museums, online, in the forest, or on the street. Given the warm embrace of our community towards our playful and idiosyncratic gallery, our minds are now attuned and our eyes open to encourage and support new artists and new artforms. We hope that the energy we have found in this project will inspire others and we encourage all to dive deep into the imagination and create innovative projects to encourage and distribute art and poetry everywhere.

-Jerry Wellman and Matthew Chase-Daniel, Axle Contemporary

Poetry in the Land of Quotidia: The Haiku Roadsign Project

Mobility, ephemerality, and a reversal of expectations are the modi operandi of Axle Contemporary, a gallery on wheels housed in a former Hostess delivery truck. It is a gallery whose location is always changing. It occupies no site in particular but has the potential to occupy any site at any time.

Like the everydayness of its vehicular host, Axle Contemporary's latest project, the Haiku Roadsign, repurposes a familiar and commercial object to provide an unexpected experience. A used roadsign, the kind that more typically announces the special or entertainment of the day for a restaurant, bar, or liquor store, conveys instead the words of poets selected by Santa Fe Poet Laureate Joan Logghe.

Because of its brevity, haiku is perhaps the most appropriate literary form to inhabit the roadsign. The Haiku Roadsign is intended to be experienced on the move—most likely by automobile, but on occasion by foot. Only a haiku can be experienced in such a fleeting way. The haiku is also a propos for a road sign because it distills much meaning through few words—an ironic twist on the same objective of advertising executives. But where advertisers' objective is earthly matters such as the pursuit of profit, the haiku's history intertwines with Zen Buddhism and thus stresses instead a freedom from worldly concerns.

No matter what your mode of mobility—by car, by train, by foot—the signs that surround us tend to enter our consciousness only when *they* are new or when *we* are new to a situation. In our daily routine, those business signs and roadsigns are so present that they are overlooked. The transience of the Haiku Roadsign, its location and content changed weekly over the course of Summer 2011, keeps it fresh in people's sight and minds. It appeared in front of an insurance office one week, another week along the Mother Road of Commercial Activity in Santa Fe (Cerrillos Road), and on the corner of the historic Plaza in front of the New Mexico Museum of Art another. Just as a haiku conveys a sense of time and place, so too do the changing haikus on the Roadsign endeavor to be specific to the sign's placement on any given week.

The Haiku Roadsign isn't exactly a guerrilla project—the authors (of the project and of each haiku) are identified clearly and it is sited by purveyors Matthew Chase-Daniel and Jerry Wellman during daylight hours, a large, heavy, rather inelegant object that is not exactly stealth to install. But to the unwitting viewer who comes upon it during his or her daily comings and goings, it is an unexpected gift—an idea or image to contemplate. If the viewer is open to receiving it as such. Indeed, response ran the spectrum, from curiosity, interest, and confusion to self-proclaimed haiku policing or disdain. That gamut of responses demonstrates that the Haiku Roadsign accomplished its purpose: to enter the passerby's consciousness and not go unseen.

The Haiku Roadsign is not an ordinary messenger, as is a message board in front of a civil building, for example. Rather, it presents itself as sculpture, albeit one that boasts a particular form and temporal nature that challenges the idea of conventional sculpture. There is no preciousness of material or craftsmanship in terms of the three-dimensional armature. Quite the opposite, in fact. It shows the wear and tear of its former life or lives and no effort has been made to hide the fact that it is an artifact of a pre-digital world. The block letters have to be added individually by hand to string together letters into words, words into haikus. Moreover, it is not the output of a single artist at work in his or her studio; rather, it is the collective effort of many: Chase-Daniel and Wellman, who organized the project; the poets who wrote the haikus and submitted them for consideration; Logghe, who selected haikus from among those submitted; and property owners who were open-minded enough to give the sculpture a home for a week.

The Axle Contemporary founders' inspiration was roadside advertising campaigns such as the Burma Shave sign series that occupied mid-century roadsides and the teaser billboards along I-10 for the multipurpose roadside attraction The Thing! in Arizona. Axle's is like other projects that co-opt the vehicles of advertising for the purpose of their own more purposeful messaging—including the MAK Center's How Many Billboards? project in Los Angeles, Albuquerque's Friends of the Orphan Signs project, or Atlanta artist John Morse's ironic remake of "bandit signs," those omnipresent small-scale signs on telephone poles that promise weight loss, quick money, or debt reduction. "We wanted to refresh the public sphere with something more interesting to see and to read," say Chase-Daniel and Wellman, "to provide a gift, a surprise, a little something for people to reflect upon as they make their way through the world." Like all Axle Contemporary projects, the Haiku Roadsign project tries to reinvent, reframe, and refresh the art experience and our day-to-day routines in what they call "the land of quotidia."

-Laura Addison, Curator of Contemporary Art, New Mexico Museum of Art

Drive Slowly: Haiku Zone

I turned into the parking lot off of Alameda and there was Elizabeth Raby's haiku:

> RENEWED
> BY NIGHT RAIN
> DOVE'S WILD CALL

and on the other side, Jenny Goldberg, a dear Taos Friend:

> EVENING PRIMROSE
> HOW DO I OPEN
> THE NIGHT

Even though we were at week nine and I had been sighting the Haiku Roadsign around town, coming upon the poems in a place I frequented stunned me. I was filled with happiness in seeing their work in broad daylight, and as if by chance. I was for a moment a stranger in my own locale, shocked awake. A small startle at 8:00 AM.

Haiku Roadsign has been this kind of joy. As Poet Laureate I was asked to judge or curate the haiku. Now there is nothing I like less than judging my friends', colleagues', and students' writing. But when I met with Matthew and Jerry I knew I was just catching the breeze of a gust of beauty. It would be my pleasure to be involved in their genius project, and they already knew I was a major Van Fan of Axle Contemporary gallery. I'd been bragging on them for months.

And haiku, I have been reading for decades. In this town there are many more practiced haiku poets, but happily we got to choose some of them for the roadsign. I am an aficionado and an amateur haiku poet. I write them, sure, and I teach them, but this time I got to be invited to influence what would be in our public psyche over the months of summer.

The work came to me anonymously on slips of paper, like large fortunes. Michael and I went out to eat at a lovely Asian Fusion restaurant. I ordered a margarita and did a quick read in the most decisive moments of my poetic life. It was as if being Poet Laureate has sharpened my sword of discernment, or maybe it was the margarita. I'd then hand them to my husband who agreed or disagreed, I didn't care. I was in the haiku zone.

The next morning, with black tea and daylight, I spent more time with them and easily picked 32 choices out of the 230 entries from nearly 100 poets. I looked for image, crisp language, freshness, and a turn or surprise. We didn't count syllables, but the sensibility of haiku is what I was after, and I have an inner haiku alarm if they get too long. In our case we were under the constraints of the lettering on the sign and asked people to keep the lines to under twenty-three letters.

The next step was meeting with Jerry and Matthew at Flying Star, our meeting spot, and identities were revealed. Sometimes disappointed that a dear friend wasn't chosen, mostly I rejoiced that so many I knew in the community were among them. It was very democratic. We got to select a wide range of poets, from beginners to some of the finest haiku poets in America. Renowned poets Miriam Sagan, John Brandi, and Charles Trumbull editor of the journal Modern Haiku are among the winners.

Having haiku out and about on the streets of Santa Fe just hits the spot for my goal of Living La Vida Local during my two-year tenure as Poet Laureate, the only tenure I am going to have in this lifetime. In an interview with High Coup Journal I called it guerilla haiku. I got interviewed two times in a week about haiku, and indeed coming upon these signs at locations as diverse as the Children's Museum, Warehouse 21, or gritty Cerrillos Road, each time I have an attack of beauty.

One quality in haiku is the reverberation, the after tones in a struck gong. My friend Judyth Hill, a great poet now living outside of San Miguel de Allende, says in a poem of hers from *Black Hollyhock, First Light*, "There's a secret in haiku, I'll tell you/ the fourth line is silent." I feel the waves of haiku ripple out into the pond of Santa Fe, like the much-translated frog of haiku maestro Matsuo Basho that keeps jumping and jumping into us for centuries.

-Joan Logghe, Santa Fe Poet Laureate

Seth T. Cohen

spring winds
everything blown
but our unraked leaves

1302 Cerrillos Road

Skip Rapoport

art is in the street
gallery walls are barren
this is just a sign

1302 Cerrillos Road

Lauren Camp

slow down
mañana still
under construction

Artisan, 2601 Cerrillos Road

Cheri Ibes

rough road ahead
alternate route advised
wander

Artisan, 2601 Cerrillos Road

Debbie Adams

swifts
gone in a flash
Santa Fe sunset

The Pecos Trail Inn, 2239 Old Pecos Trail

Dara Mark

Under the pinon
that blue shadow
left behind again

The Pecos Trail Inn, 2239 Old Pecos Trail

Marian Olson

ripples of heat
a snake slips under
the front porch

Santa Fe Auto Repair, 2650 Sawmill Road

Stella Reed

sound of your breathing
makes me long
for ice cream in bed

Santa Fe Auto Repair, 2650 Sawmill Road

Teresa Gallion

Showers tease desert
Water droplets hangout
Hip hop in sand

Rader Awning, 1305 South Saint Francis Drive

Wayne Lee

My bicycle chain
is broken. Sitting still is
good as getting there.

Rader Awning, 1305 South Saint Francis Drive

Rick Smith

Three plastic daisies:
A faded, sad *descanso*
But, *yo recuerdo*

Café Olé, 2411 Cerrillos Road

Dru Philippou

gifts from my mother
unwrapping them
with their shadows

Café Olé, 2411 Cerrillos Road

Jane Lipman

in all the windows
of the world
one moon

Santa Fe Children's Museum, 1050 Old Pecos Trail

John Brandi

axle repair—-
from under the chassis
the full moon

Santa Fe Children's Museum, 1050 Old Pecos Trail

John Knoll

Just one chord
Maria's voice
A choir

Barbara Robidoux

on the envelope
of your dear John letter
a forever stamp

Warehouse 21, 1614 Paseo de Peralta

Jenny Goldberg

evening primrose
how do I open
the night

James Armijo State Farm Insurance, 901 West Alameda Street

Elizabeth Raby

renewed
by night rain
dove's wild call

James Armijo State Farm Insurance, 901 West Alameda Street

N. Scott Momaday

the old couple walk
through the gardens of their youth
with no thought of time

New Mexico Museum of Art, 107 West Palace Avenue

Katherine Shelton

Wherever I am
A vast tent of sky
My own circus show

New Mexico Museum of Art, 107 West Palace Avenue

Brian Leekley

Feeling vertigo
as on the edge of a cliff,
I look in your eyes.

Barker Realty, 530 S Guadalupe Street

Deborah A. Cole

Who among us inhaled
the cloud that hid
last night's moon?

Barker Realty, 530 S Guadalupe Street

Sandra D. Lynn

The roadrunner
His iridescent eye
Is on me

Santa Fe Woman's Club, 1616 Old Pecos Trail

Grace Henderson

A powerful source
And so the happiness flows-
One of the people

Santa Fe Woman's Club, 1616 Old Pecos Trail

Susan Swab

Teenagers walking along
wild horses grazing
rocking chair waits.

Railyard Park, Cerrillos Road

Miriam Sagan

you tell me these ducks
don't always mate for life--are
you flirting with me?

Railyard Park, Cerrillos Road

Charles Trumbull

Ghost Ranch
the silent passage
of a crow

Lamplighter Inn, 2405 Cerrillos Road

Eve De Bona

dried cow parsnips…
a spider enlaces them
with threads of silver

Lamplighter Inn, 2405 Cerrillos Road

Burning Books

follow the arrow
infinity just ahead
happy hour starts now

Railyard Park, Guadalupe Street

Don McIver

What a hangover!
Even the constellations
are really bright.

Railyard Park, Guadalupe Street

Ursula Moeller

horses stand quiet
mountains chill breath
shifting vapor clouds

Los Chile Bros, 3140 Cerrillos Road

Marguerite Wilson

smarting eyes
chiles roasting
fall on Cerrillos road

Los Chile Bros, 3140 Cerrillos Road

Poet Biographies

Debbie Adams of Santa Fe, is a member of the Haiku Society of America and has published in Modern Haiku, the HSA Anthology 2011, the Anthology of English Language Haiku by Women and the Small Canyon Review.

Eve De Bona is a visual artist and poet who has settled in Santa Fe after living the past ten years in Oaxaca, Mexico.

John Brandi, poet, painter and essayist, has lived in New Mexico forty years. He has been writing haiku since 1980, much of it collected into his latest book, *Seeding the Cosmos* (La Alameda Press, 2010).

Burning Books is better at making the world more elegant and convincing when it operates as a low-key dysfunctional entity.

Lauren Camp is allergic to eggs and boredom. An arts educator, visual artist, and KSFR radio host, she is also the author of a book of poems: *This Business of Wisdom*. She blogs about poetry everyday.

Seth Tucker Cohen's creative impulses are largely repressed during normal business hours when he serves as an Assistant Attorney General, protecting New Mexico's air and water. He lives in Santa Fe with his wife and daughter.

During 3 decades in New Mexico, **Deborah A. Cole** has explored printmaking, painting, sculpture, artists' books, memoir, and haiku. She has left artwork in the landscape for years; these are her first words to find their way there.

Teresa E. Gallion's poetry appears in numerous journals and anthologies as well as a CD and chapbook. The surreal high desert landscape and her personal spiritual journey influence the writing of this Albuquerque poet.

Jenny Goldberg lives on a sunny windy mesa above Taos with her two dogs. Her poems live in Adobe Walls, Blue Mesa Review, Malpaís Review, Passager, Rio Grande Review and Sin Fronteras.

Grace Henderson is a student at the Academy for Technology and the Classics in Santa Fe. She likes the 80's.

Cheri Ibes is a visual artist living in Santa Fe. This is her first foray into haiku.

John Knoll, editor/owner of PojoaqueNews.com an online news site, has lived in Pojoaque, N.M. for the past 26 years. He has published five poetry books and a CD with John Macker.

Wayne Lee lives with his wife, poet/painter Alice Lee, in Santa Fe, where he teaches at DeVargas Middle School. His third book of poems, *Leap, Float*, is forthcoming from Red Mountain Press.

Brian Leekley is a novelist and a retired antiquarian bookseller. He and his wife, artist Kayle Rice, have been Santa Feans since November 2010.

Jane Lipman's chapbooks, The *Rapture of Tulips* and *White Crow's Secret Life* (Pudding House Publications), were finalists for N.M. Book Awards in Poetry in 2009 and 2010, respectively. She is completing a full-length collection.

Sandra Lynn has lived in New Mexico since 1988. She has published three books (poetry and nonfiction) and many poems, essays, articles, and photographs. She enjoys and practices two Japanese art forms--haiku and ikebana.

Dara Mark is primarily a painter whose work has sometimes been called "visual haiku."

Don McIver has performed all over the United States, produced poetry events big and small, and been published in numerous magazines and anthologies.

Ursula Moeller was born in Vienna, Austria, spent WWII in Cambridge, England, emigrated to NY, lived 40+ years in Syracuse NY, is now in Santa Fe for 14 years, and plans to stay here forever.

N. Scott Momaday has published numerous poems and other writings. He has been awarded a Pulitzer Prize and the National Medal for the Arts. He resides in Florida and New Mexico.

Marian Olson of Santa Fe, is the author of *Songs of the Chicken Yard*, an acclaimed book of haiku and senryu, and *Desert Hours*, which won first place in the Merit Books Awards of 2008: a finalist in the 2008 N.M. Book Awards.

Dru Philippou's work has appeared in numerous journals. He was nominated for the Puscart Prize, and has been been acknowledged by the Scorpion, Roadrunner, R. Spiess, J. Kilbride, and Vancouver Cherry Blossom contests.

Elizabeth Raby has lived in Santa Fe since 2000. She is the author of two full-length collections, *Ink on Snow*, 2010, and *The Year the Pears Bloomed Twice*, 2009, both published by Virtual Artists Collective, and four chapbooks.

Skip Rapoport is a Santa Fe based lighting designer for Theatre and Dance. This is not nearly as cool as his current (part-time) gig as a roadsign poet.

Stella Reed has been living, writing, singing and loving in northern New Mexico for over 23 years. Her favorite ice cream is actually chocolate lavender gelato, but that has too many syllables.

Barbara Robidoux lives in Santa Fe. She has published one book of poetry *Waiting for Rain* and is currently working on a collection of haiku, tanka and haibun.

Miriam Sagan founded and directs the creative writing program at Santa Fe Community College, and curates the permanent installation of Poetry Posts there. She won the 2010 Santa Fe mayor's award for excellence in the arts.

Katherine Shelton's big loves are pottery, poetry, painting, grandchildren, gardens, hiking, bicycling, birds, mountains, oceans, and coffee. New Mexico blessed since 1979.

Rick Smith is a reformed whitewater boater and river guide. He lives in Santa Fe with his wife Layne and three cats, Chica, Cuate, and Reina.

Susan Swab: Creativity opens her heart, travel expands her mind, money offers her choices, sitting still, listening and breathing bring her peace.

Charles Trumbull, who grew up in New Mexico and now lives in Santa Fe, is retired from Encyclopaedia Britannica in Chicago. He edits the journal Modern Haiku.

Marguerite Wilson is a former debutante, ski instructor, hippie, and tennis player, current fiber artist, philosopher, vaastu consultant, apronista, peace activist, ayurvedic student, mentor, Nia enthusiast, and lover of life.

www.ingramcontent.com/pod-product-compliance
Lightning Source LLC
Chambersburg PA
CBHW042025150426
43198CB00002B/70